JUV/
QB
331
.N34
2003

ORIOLE

Chicago Public Library

W9-BLR-573

Oriole Park Branch
7454 W. Balmoral Ave.
60656

DISCARD

The KidHaven Science Library

Gravity

by Don Nardo

KIDHAVEN
PRESS™

THOMSON

———✦———™

GALE

San Diego • Detroit • New York • San Francisco • Cleveland
New Haven, Conn. • Waterville, Maine • London • Munich

THOMSON

GALE

™

Cover photo: © Duomo/CORBIS
© Archivo Iconographico, S.A./CORBIS, 10
© Bettmann/CORBIS, 8
© Chris Bjornberg/Photo Researchers, Inc., 16
© C. Butler/Photo Researchers, Inc., 21
© CORBIS, 28, 34
© Digital Art/CORBIS, 39
© Myron Jay Dorf/CORBIS, 30
© David A. Hardy/Photo Researchers, Inc., 7
© Roger Harris/Photo Researchers, Inc., 26
Chris Jouan, 38
Mary Evans Picture Library, 36
© NASA/CORBIS, 22

Brandy Noon, 29
© Charles O'Rear/CORBIS, 19
PhotoDisc, 24, 35
© Bill Sanderson/Photo Researchers, Inc., 15
© Science Photo Library/Photo Researchers,
    Inc., 12
© Richard Hamilton Smith/CORBIS, 5
© Space Telescope Science
    Institute/NASA/Photo Researchers, Inc., 31
© James A. Sugar/CORBIS, 18
© Victor Habbick Visions/Photo Researchers,
    Inc., 41

© 2003 by KidHaven Press. KidHaven Press is an imprint of The Gale Group, Inc.,
a division of Thomson Learning, Inc.

KidHaven™ and Thomson Learning™ are trademarks used herein under license.

For more information, contact
KidHaven Press
27500 Drake Rd.
Farmington Hills, MI 48331-3535
Or you can visit our Internet site at http://www.gale.com

ALL RIGHTS RESERVED.
No part of this work covered by the copyright hereon may be reproduced or used in any form
or by any means—graphic, electronic, or mechanical, including photocopying, recording, taping,
Web distribution or information storage retrieval systems—without the written permission of
the publisher.

LIBRARY OF CONGRESS CATALOGING-IN-PUBLICATION DATA

Nardo, Don, 1947–
    Gravity : by Don Nardo.
        p. cm. — (The Kidhaven science library)
    Includes index.
    Summary: Discusses early theories on gravity, principles of how gravity works,
and possible effects of gravity with regard to such phenomena as white dwarfs
and black holes.
    ISBN 0-7377-1404-2 (hbk. : alk. paper)
    1. Gravity—Juvenile literature. 2. Gravitation—Juvenile literature.   [1. Gravity.]
I. Title. II. Series.
QB331 .N34 2003
531' .14—dc21
                                                          2002013085

Printed in the United States of America

R0402197742

Oriole Park Branch
~~Balmoral~~
Chicago, IL 60656

DISCARD

Contents

Chapter 1

The Long Road to Gravity's Discovery

Just about everyone takes the existence of **gravity** for granted. No one can see it, of course, because it is an invisible force. Yet its effects can be seen and felt. When a ball or other object is thrown, for example, it always falls back to Earth. Sky divers or bungie jumpers plummet downward at great speed until a parachute or bungie cord breaks their fall. And the moon endlessly circles Earth, held tightly in gravity's strong embrace.

These are examples of the effects of Earth's gravity. Our planet is not the only body that has a gravitational pull, however. In fact, all objects in the **universe**, both large and small, have gravity. Not surprisingly, the bigger an object is, the larger its gravitational pull. Thus, Earth's gravity keeps pebbles, people, houses, mountains, and the moon from floating away into space. And the sun, which is thousands of times larger than Earth, holds Earth and the other planets in the **solar system** in orbit around it. (The solar system consists of the sun and all the planets, moons, comets, and other bodies that move around it.) In short, gravity directs the motions of all objects everywhere, from tiny pebbles to gigantic stars.

A Geocentric View

Because people tend to take gravity for granted, it is easy to forget that no one knew of its existence until a few hundred years ago. In past ages, people could see the sun, moon, and planets moving through the sky. But early scientists and other thinkers based their explanations for these motions on faulty ideas. For instance, they commonly accepted the

Roller coasters depend on gravity to pull the riders downward with great force.

notion that Earth lies at the center of all things and the heavenly bodies move around Earth. This came to be called the **geocentric** view of the universe.

Aristotle

The long road to gravity's discovery began with one of the main supporters of the geocentric view. He was the ancient Greek thinker Aristotle. Aristotle's ideas strongly influenced scholars and religious leaders for nearly two thousand years. Aristotle had a clever explanation for the motions of the heavenly bodies, motions now known to be caused by gravity. Something must hold these bodies in their orbits above Earth, he reasoned. He proposed that a series of invisible spheres (globes) floated in the sky. Each planet or other heavenly body rested on the surface of its own sphere. Moreover, the various spheres lay inside one another, with Earth, also a sphere, resting at the center.

Aristotle also considered the effects caused by Earth-based gravity. Like everyone else, he saw that an object thrown into the air always falls back down. But he did not connect this kind of motion with the movements of the heavenly bodies. He simply accepted the idea of falling bodies as a natural occurrence.

The Sun-Centered View

Most later ancient scientists accepted and passed on Aristotle's ideas. There was little chance of anyone

In the early years of the solar system, the sun and planets formed under the influence of gravity.

discovering gravity and how it works until scientists first recognized that the geocentric view was wrong. This finally happened in the late 1500s and early 1600s. In 1543, Polish astronomer Nicolaus Copernicus published his groundbreaking work, *On the*

Polish astronomer Nicolaus Copernicus created a stir in Europe when he declared that the Earth is not the center of all things.

Revolutions. Using mathematics and logic, he showed that Earth does not lie at the center of things. Instead, it is just one of several planets. And along with the other planets, Earth moves around the sun. This became known as the **heliocentric** view.

Soon another scientist, an Italian priest named Giordano Bruno, took Copernicus's ideas a step further. Bruno said that the stars visible in the night sky are really other suns. And like the sun, each might have planets of its own. Furthermore, the same natural force that keeps Earth in orbit around the sun holds the planets of distant suns in their orbits. Bruno did not name this force, which people now call gravity. Perhaps he might have gone on to propose the first major theory of gravity. Unfortunately, though, church leaders declared that his ideas were against God and the teachings of the Bible, and were therefore dangerous. They burned him at the stake in the year 1600.

Galileo

The church could order a person's death. But it could not destroy an idea whose time had come. Not long after Bruno's death, another Italian thinker, Galileo Galilei, became the first person to use a new device, the telescope, to study the night sky. In 1610, Galileo discovered the four largest moons of Jupiter. Night after night, he watched them move around the planet. And it seemed to

To learn more about gravity, Galileo (right) conducted important experiments with falling weights.

him that Jupiter must be exerting some unknown force to keep those moons in orbit.

Galileo also conducted experiments with weights to see if heavy objects fall faster than lighter ones. Galileo found that all objects fall at the same rate, regardless of weight. However, he, too, did not realize that the force that holds moons in their orbits is the same force that causes objects to fall on Earth.

The first major theory of gravity made that vital connection. It was proposed in the late 1600s by the brilliant English scientist Isaac Newton. He claimed he first got the idea from watching an apple fall from a tree. Like Galileo and other earlier scientists, Newton knew that Earth draws objects such as apples and people toward its center. Newton also knew that Earth pulls on the moon, and the sun pulls on Earth. It occurred to him that a single force might be affecting all these bodies. Furthermore, this mysterious force, which he called gravity, might be a property of *all* objects, no matter how big or small.

This made sense to Newton because all objects, big or small, or near or far, have one thing in common: all have **mass.** That is, each consists of a measurable amount of matter. In fact, he said, the force of gravity exerted by an object is directly related to the amount of its mass. A small object, such as a chair, has very little mass. So it exerts very little gravitational pull and does not attract nearby objects. In contrast, a very large object, such as a planet, has a great amount of mass. So its gravity is capable of attracting chairs, people, mountains, and moons.

Gravity Relates to Distance

The force of gravity is also related to distance, Newton showed. The farther apart two objects are, the less their gravities attract each other. The closer two objects are, the stronger they attract each other.

The sun lies at the center of the solar system, which is made up of planets, moons, and many other smaller bodies.

Thus, Earth easily maintains its hold on the moon, which is relatively near. But Earth's gravity has no measurable effect on the planet Mars, which is much farther away. Of course, if Earth had enough mass, it *could* attract Mars. That is why the sun is able to hold Mars in orbit. The sun is much farther away from Mars than Earth is. But the sun is also much more massive than Earth is.

Newton concluded correctly that gravity works the same in all parts of the universe. So when he developed a mathematical formula showing how gravity works, he called it the law of universal gravitation. Later, scientists used the formula to measure the masses of the sun, planets, and moons. They also used it to explain and predict planetary motions. In addition, Newton's theory of gravity perfectly explains the motions of objects on Earth. Thus, Newton demonstrated that a single mathematical law can explain the motions of all the bodies in nature.

Living with Gravity on Earth

Isaac Newton showed how gravity controls the motions of the heavenly bodies. But calculating the masses and orbits of planets and moons was the concern of only scientists. The average person was (and still is) interested in gravity only as it affects or might someday affect his or her daily life.

Years, Months, and Days

One important way that gravity affects life on Earth is the indirect role it plays in keeping time. Consider the example of the year, the amount of time it takes Earth to revolve around the sun once. A year lasts 365 days partly because of the relationship between the masses of the sun and Earth. If Earth's mass were a little different, the sun's gravity would pull on it differently. In that case, Earth might lie a little closer to or a little farther away from the sun than it does now. And if so, a year would be slightly shorter or slightly longer. Similarly, a month is a measure of the amount of time it takes the moon to move around Earth once. As in the case of a year, the length of a month would be different if the moon were more or less massive than it is.

In fact, the length of the month *has* been different in the past and will continue to change in the future. The reason is the changing effects of gravity caused by the moon's large mass and closeness to

English scientist Isaac Newton developed a formula for gravity that factors in the masses of objects and the distances between them.

Earth. Over time, the pull of their two gravities has slowed the rate at which each rotates, or spins, on its axis. The moon still rotates. But its period of rotation exactly equals its period of revolution around Earth. So the moon forever keeps the same side facing Earth.

At the same time, the pull of the moon's gravity is causing Earth's rotation to slow. The length of a day on Earth is growing longer by a very tiny amount

The moon (right) always keeps the same side facing Earth.

each century. Many millions of years from now, Earth and moon will be locked in a strange embrace. A day on Earth will last fifty times longer than it does today. Meanwhile, the moon will no longer rotate. It will move around Earth in the same period—fifty days. In this odd situation, a day and a month will be the same length. Also, to a person living on the side of Earth facing the moon, that object will forever remain fixed in the same spot in the sky. And a person living on the other side of Earth will never see the moon at all.

The Tides

The moon's presence and movement around Earth do more than determine the length of the month and day. The moon's gravity also causes the tides. As the moon moves along in its orbit, its gravity pulls on Earth's oceans. And the water bulges slightly on both the side facing the moon and the side facing away from it. As Earth rotates, the tidal bulges move across its surface. And when they reach the edges of the land masses, the water crawls up the shores in the form of high tides. Because there are two tidal bulges, high tide occurs twice a day.

The sun's gravity also contributes to the tides. But because our star is so far away, its tidal force on Earth is only about one-third of the moon's. Still, the sun's gravity has taken a toll over time. In the past 4.5 billion years, sun-generated tides have caused the

The tidal bulges created by the sun and moon move across the Earth's surface, causing high tides in coastal regions.

seas to scrape along the bottoms of the ocean basins. This has contributed slightly to the slowing of Earth's rate of rotation (although the moon's gravity has played a much larger role in this process). Together, the moon's and sun's gravities have caused the day to lengthen from six to twenty-four hours.

Earthly Disasters Caused by Gravity

Fortunately, the gravity-generated tides rarely harm people or animals. By contrast, gravity does sometimes pose a danger to earthly life by causing space debris to rain down on the planet. The solar system is littered with asteroids, made of metal or rock, and comets, made of rock and ice. These objects range in size from a few feet wide to several miles across. And from time to time Earth's or the moon's gravity pulls one of them dangerously close to Earth. The impact of even a small asteroid striking Earth's surface could destroy a city. And large impacts could kill millions of people and animals.

Barringer Crater in Arizona is one of the youngest and most distinct impact craters on Earth.

Impact Craters

The question is not whether an asteroid or comet could or might strike Earth. Such impacts have occurred many times in the past. Cosmic objects have struck both Earth and the moon, as shown by the existence of **impact craters** on both bodies. The moon's craters have survived intact because that body has no air or water to erode them (wear them down). In contrast, the effects of rain, wind, tides, volcanoes, and so forth have eroded and erased most of Earth's craters. One of the few easily visible impact craters remaining on Earth's surface lies near Winslow, Arizona. Known as Barringer Crater (or Meteor Crater), it is about three-quarters of a mile wide and six hundred feet deep. It formed about twenty-five thousand years ago. Luckily, no people were killed in the explosion because no humans lived in Arizona at the time.

However, the dinosaurs were not so fortunate. About 65 million years ago, gravity caused a far larger asteroid to collide with Earth. The object was about six miles in diameter. It struck the ocean near the eastern coast of Mexico with devastating force. It blasted out a crater more than one hundred miles across and several miles deep. The disaster wiped out about 70 percent of all the animal and plant species on the planet, including the dinosaurs.

Scientists are concerned not only with gravity pulling objects down from space, but also with

A Tyrannosaurus rex *is startled by the impact of the asteroid that will cause the dinosaurs to become extinct.*

ways to push objects *away* from Earth and *into* space. In the twentieth century, humanity finally realized the longtime dream of space flight. But this was possible only after Newton's explanation of gravity and the many experiments that occurred in the more than three centuries that followed.

The chief goal of these experiments was to allow a rocket-powered craft to escape the bonds of

American astronauts train in a special airplane that mimics the weightless conditions they will encounter in space.

Earth's gravity. To achieve this, the craft needed to reach the planet's **escape velocity**. This is the speed a body needs to move to escape the gravity of another body. Calculations based on Newton's formula show that the escape velocity of Earth is about seven miles per second. So rockets carrying satellites or people are designed to reach that speed. This allows them to break free of Earth's gravity. Thus knowledge of gravity and its workings has helped make it possible for humans to explore the wonders of outer space.

The Force That Rules the Heavens

When human-built spacecraft escape the pull of Earth's gravity, they are not completely free of gravity. Craft landing on and taking off from the moon must deal with that body's gravity. And the same will be true of trips to other planets, as well as to large asteroids and comets. In addition, all spacecraft traveling within the solar system must factor in the effects of the sun's powerful gravity. Gravity also controls the motions of heavenly bodies lying far beyond the sun's family. The same force that tugs on a rocket attempting to leave Earth rules all of the objects in the far reaches of the universe.

Gravity Creates the Sun

Indeed, gravity's rule over stars, planets, and other heavenly bodies is so complete that it begins before they are even born. In fact, it plays the key role in their creation. One example is the birth of the sun and other members of the solar system. Scientists believe that the sun began as a huge cloud of gases and dust floating through space. At first, these substances were spread out thinner than the air that people and animals breathe today. The substances were also very light. But like all matter, they exerted

The sun's surface gives off violent swirls of hot gases.

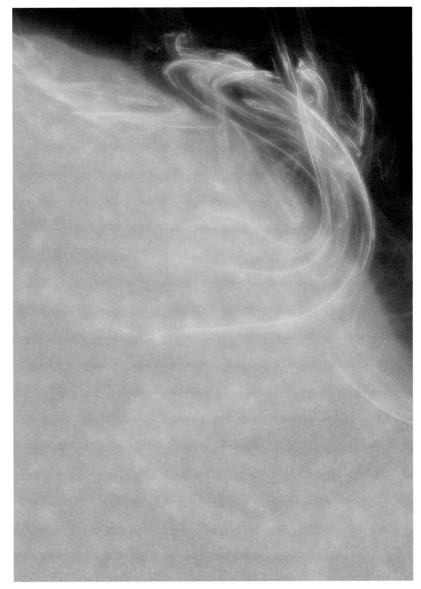

a gravitational pull, however small. As gravity attracted the particles of gas and dust to one another, very slowly the cloud began to contract. Over time it became very **dense**, or compact. This process gave off heat, so the cloud began to warm up.

For several million years the cloud continued to grow smaller, more compact, and warmer. And driven by the tireless tug of gravity, the process speeded up. Most of the gases and dust made their way into a very dense and hot central core. The rest of the material spun around the core, flattening out into a disk. After millions of years the central core finally got hot enough to ignite nuclear reactions. Then, in a blinding flash of light, the sun was born.

Planetesimals

Meanwhile, the new star's gravity still kept the disk of gases and dust spinning around it. The hot materials in the inner parts of the disk were closer to the sun. But the outer sections were cooler. So they began to solidify, or harden, into small particles of rock and ice. Driven by gravity, these particles soon began to stick to one another, creating larger pieces. This process, called **accretion**, works somewhat like building a snowman. Beginning with a small handful of snow, as it is rolled along the ground more and more snow sticks to it. This causes it to grow bigger and bigger until a huge ball of snow has formed.

In a similar manner, solid particles in the disk formed larger and larger clumps. Scientists call the

Asteroids orbit the distant sun. Many asteroids are leftover planetesimals from the solar system's earliest days.

clumps that measured between a few thousand feet and several miles **planetesimals**. Large planetesimals had enough gravity to begin pulling in even more matter. So these quickly grew into massive objects. The biggest of these objects became the planets. Several of the slightly smaller chunks went into orbit around the planets, becoming their moons. Meanwhile, most of the leftover planetesimals continued orbiting the sun as asteroids and comets. In this way, a single process set in motion by gravity resulted in the great variety of objects in the solar system.

Gravity and the Sun's Fate

Just as it did in the solar system's creation, gravity will play a key role in the fate of the sun, its family of planets, and any life on those planets. As long as the sun remains stable, it will go on shining and providing Earth with light and warmth. An average star such as the sun typically remains stable for billions of years. This is possible because two strong forces at work within the star oppose and balance each other. The first of these forces is gravity, which causes the huge amount of matter in the star's outer layers to press inward with enormous power.

The second force at work inside the sun is the outward flow of energy from the core. The nuclear reactions occurring there release immense amounts of heat, light, and tiny particles. Each and every second, the sun's core creates energy equal to that released by 100 million nuclear bombs. This huge stream of energy travels outward from the core. And as it does, it exerts a great amount of outward pressure. As it happens, the force of energy pushing outward balances the force of gravity pushing inward. So the sun maintains its structure and remains stable.

After several billion years, however, the sun will run out of the elements that fuel the nuclear reactions in its core. When that happens, the delicate balance that keeps the star stable will be upset. The outward pressure of escaping energy will weaken.

This will allow it to be overcome by the inward pressure of gravity. At that point, disaster will be certain. Some of the star's outer material will escape into space. But most will collapse inward with extreme violence. The forces involved will be so great they will crush most of the matter into a small ball about the size of Earth.

Astronomers call such an object a **white dwarf**. A white dwarf is so dense that a tablespoon of its material weighs a thousand tons. And its escape velocity is about three thousand miles per second! When the sun becomes a white dwarf, Earth will continue to orbit around it. But a white dwarf gives

Hot gases burst from the sun's surface. Someday gravity will cause the sun to collapse into a small dense object.

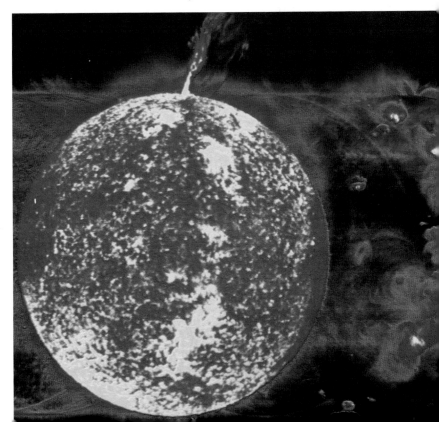

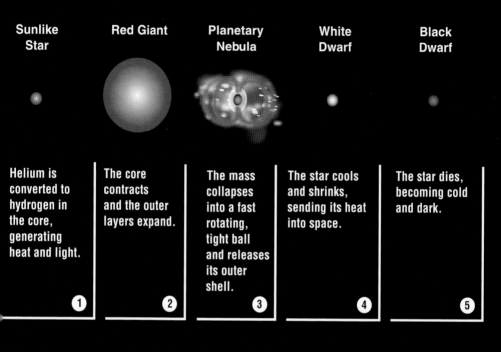

Death of the Sun

Sunlike Star	Red Giant	Planetary Nebula	White Dwarf	Black Dwarf
Helium is converted to hydrogen in the core, generating heat and light.	The core contracts and the outer layers expand.	The mass collapses into a fast rotating, tight ball and releases its outer shell.	The star cools and shrinks, sending its heat into space.	The star dies, becoming cold and dark.
1	2	3	4	5

off very little energy and almost no heat, so the Earth's surface will quickly freeze over. And all life will cease to exist.

Galaxies and Superclusters

Gravity has been creating and destroying stars this way for a long time. And this process will continue far into the future. Meanwhile, during the billions of years that stars remain stable, their motions are constantly guided by gravity's invisible hand. Our own star does not stand still in space, for example. Together with other stars, the sun, carrying along its family, orbits the center of the local **galaxy**. A galaxy is a gigantic group of billions of stars all held together by their gravitational attractions.

Astronomers call our home galaxy the Milky Way. It is so huge that trying to express its size in standard units of measure such as miles or kilometers is confusing. So astronomers use a special and much larger unit called a **light year**. A light year is the distance that light travels in a year, or about 6 trillion miles. The Milky Way is a big, more or less circular disk about one hundred thousand light years across and

From a great distance, the Milky Way would look something like this neighboring galaxy.

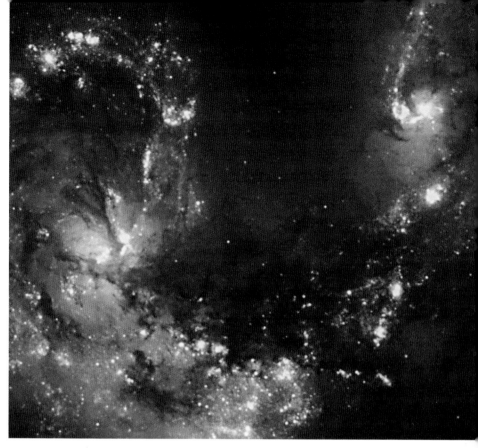

Drawn together by gravity, these two distant galaxies collided and passed through each other in the recent past.

seven thousand light years thick. Its stars orbit its center in large spiral arms. So if one could view the Milky Way from high above, it would look somewhat like a giant pinwheel.

The solar system is located in one of the Milky Way's spiral arms at a distance of about twenty-six thousand light years from the center. Held fast by gravity, the sun and its family move around that center very quickly. By one estimate, they speed along at about 136 miles per second. Still, even at that rate it takes the solar system more than 200 million years to orbit the galaxy once. The sun and its planets are estimated to be about 4.5 billion years old. So they have made at least nineteen trips around the galaxy's center to date.

Incredibly, gravity's rule does not end at the outer edges of the Milky Way. Our galaxy is only one among billions that stretch outward in all directions as far as the largest telescopes can see. Each galaxy uses gravity to control the motions of its own family of stars. And on an even larger scale, gravity often draws separate galaxies toward one another. Astronomers have detected enormous clusters of galaxies moving through space. These in turn form even larger groups of galaxies called superclusters. In short, throughout the universe gravity's influence is limitless.

Chapter 4

Gravity Wells and Galactic Monsters

So far, gravity has been considered mainly as it works under ordinary conditions. But what happens with gravity under *extra*ordinary conditions? A hint can be seen in the case of a white dwarf. When an average star such as the sun runs out of fuel and collapses inward on itself, its matter gets crushed into an unusually dense object—a white dwarf.

But white dwarfs are not the densest objects in the universe. And they are far from the strangest. Some stars are even larger than the sun. They have more mass and much stronger gravities. So their collapse is more violent and creates an object even more dense than a white dwarf. Scientists call such an object a **neutron star**. A tablespoon of neutron star material weighs at least several trillion tons. And its escape velocity is nearly 125,000 miles per second, about two-thirds the speed of light. (The speed of light is about 186,000 miles per second.) That means that a spacecraft sitting on the surface of a neutron star would have to attain a speed of 125,000 miles per second to break free of the object's gravity!

Because light is just barely able to escape from a neutron star, the gravity of an even denser object would keep light from escaping. Such superdense objects do exist. They are known as **black holes**. A black hole forms from the collapse of a star that is many times the mass of the sun. With a black hole the force of the collapse is so huge that it does not stop at the white dwarf or neutron star stages. Instead, the gravity-driven inward rush of matter continues on and on. Atoms are ripped apart and their remnants packed tightly together. The final result is an object so dense and massive that its escape velocity is greater than the speed of light. Simply put, a black hole's gravity is so great that even light cannot escape it. And that is why it appears black.

The strong gravity of a neutron star pulls gases off of the object's companion star.

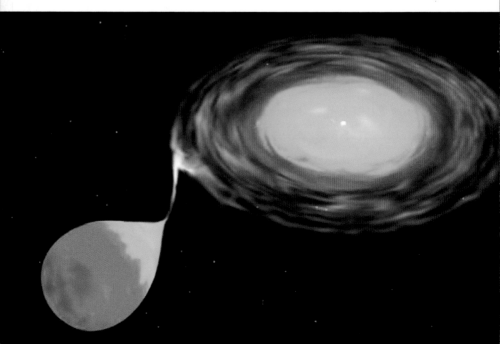

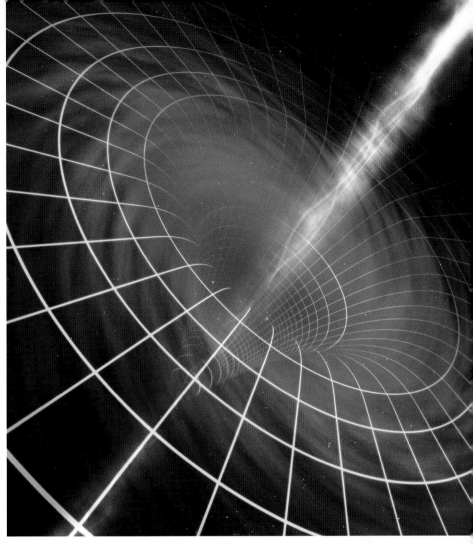

An artist offers a view of the steep and very deep gravity well of a black hole.

The Strange Case of Curved Space

Black holes are more than superdense objects with tremendously strong gravities, however. These objects also distort the very fabric of space. Before the twentieth century, scientists did not even know

The 4 Equations

$$g_{ik,l} = 0; \quad \Gamma_i^l = 0$$

$$R_{ik} = 0; \quad g_{,s}^{is} = 0$$

The great German scientist Albert Einstein suggested that gravity is a property of the bendable fabric of space.

that space *has* a fabric. They assumed that it is just an empty void having no ability to affect the objects that move within it.

Then, in the early years of the century, a brilliant German scientist named Albert Einstein proposed a new theory of matter and gravity. His ideas forever changed the way humans view space and the objects within it. Einstein explained the workings of gravity differently than Newton had. Newton had described gravity as a force exerted by objects. In contrast, Einstein argued that gravity is a property of space itself. Space has some invisible properties, he said, among them a fabric with an elastic, or bendable, quality. Furthermore, he stated, objects with mass that are moving through space interact with this hidden fabric. Such an object sinks into the fabric, creating a depression in it. Also, the more massive the object is, the deeper the depression. Thus, very massive objects distort, or curve, the fabric of space. And this curvature is what people experience as gravity.

Consider two planets of different sizes approaching each other. The smaller planet encounters the curve of the larger object's depression, or **gravity well**. Soon, the smaller planet rolls "downhill" toward the larger one. This is equivalent to the larger planet "pulling in" the smaller one in Newtonian terms. If the smaller planet is moving fast enough, it can roll back out of the other's gravity well and escape. If not, it remains trapped. And it either orbits around or crashes into the larger planet.

The Threat Posed by Black Holes

A natural question to ask is: How dangerous are these supermassive objects created by the extreme effects of gravity? The answer is that it depends on how close one gets to one. Any planet orbiting a star that collapses into a black hole would be doomed. Most living things would die from powerful radiation released during the star's collapse. And any survivors would freeze to death after the star ceased giving off light and heat.

Luckily, though, these deadly effects would not reach very far beyond the general region of the black hole. The distances between most stars are very great—usually many trillions of miles. So black holes that form this way would pose little or no threat to neighboring stars and their planets. Only

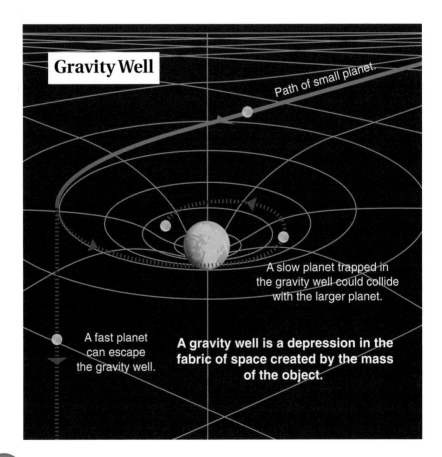

Gravity Well

Path of small planet.

A slow planet trapped in the gravity well could collide with the larger planet.

A fast planet can escape the gravity well.

A gravity well is a depression in the fabric of space created by the mass of the object.

Gases swirl around a large black hole, which lies hidden in the center of the vortex.

in regions where many large stars lie very close together would the danger increase. Then a black hole might suck in neighboring stars and planets, and over time it would grow much larger. In a sense it would become a monster with a huge appetite.

Recent evidence shows that such cosmic monsters do exist. Astronomers have devoted much attention to the cores of galaxies, including that of the Milky Way. Indeed, new and very large telescopes and other advanced instruments have revealed a great deal about our galaxy's core. There, many huge stars lie very close together. Some of these stars are 120 times the size of the sun or larger. Most are moving very rapidly around a massive object in the center of the core. The object, called Sagittarius A-star, has about 2.6 million times the sun's mass. Most scientists now believe it is a supermassive black hole. Astronomers have detected similar objects in the centers of many other galaxies.

The Ultimate Fate of Galaxies

Sagittarius A-star has already pulled in and consumed more than 2 million stars. And it will likely continue to grow. Indeed, evidence shows that the supermassive black holes in many other galaxies are much larger. Andromeda, the nearest major galaxy to our Milky Way, has an object in its core that is 30 million times heavier than the sun. And in the center of a galaxy dubbed NGC 4261 lies an object with 1.2 billion times the sun's mass!

This suggests that there is no limit to how big a black hole can get. In fact, the ultimate fate of galaxies and the living things within them may be decided by these supermassive monsters. Consider the one lurking in the Milky Way's core. It is possible that several billion years from now, its gravity will suck in all the stars in the galaxy. If so, it will draw our own solar system, including Earth, into its black

In this artist's view, the planets of a distant star system are steadily sucked into the mouth of a giant black hole.

mouth. The sun, planets, moons, and everything else will be crushed and ripped apart. Reduced to atoms, they will spiral into the black hole, adding to its growing mass.

Fortunately, if human beings still exist in that far future they will have plenty of warning of the coming disaster. Long before it, they may move to stars lying farther from the galactic core. Or perhaps they will possess the technology to travel to another, younger galaxy. Or maybe they will be so advanced that they will be able to control the galactic monster and use it to their advantage. If so, gravity, creator and destroyer of stars, will be tamed by an even greater power—that of the human mind.

Gravity Wells and Galactic Monsters

accretion: A process in which small pieces of a substance stick together to form larger pieces.

black holes: Superdense objects with gravity so strong that not even light can escape them.

curved space: The concept, first advanced by German scientist Albert Einstein, that space has an invisible fabric that bends when objects with mass move through it.

dense: Highly compact.

escape velocity: The speed that a body needs to move to escape the gravity of another body.

galaxy: A gigantic group of stars held together by their mutual gravities. Our galaxy is called the Milky Way.

geocentric: Earth-centered.

gravity: A force exerted by an object that attracts other objects. The pull of Earth's gravity keeps rocks, people, and houses from floating away into space. It also holds the moon in its orbit around Earth.

gravity well: A depression in the fabric of space created by the mass of an object. The more massive the object, the deeper the well.

heliocentric: Sun-centered.

impact crater: A hole in the ground created by the crash of an asteroid or other object from space.

light year: The distance that light travels in a year, or about 6 trillion miles.

mass: The measurable matter making up an object.

neutron star: A superdense object that forms from the collapse of a large star.

planetesimals: Small objects that orbited the early sun and combined to form the planets.

solar system: The sun and all the planets, moons, asteroids, and other objects held by the sun's gravity.

universe: The sum total of all the space and matter known to exist.

white dwarf: A superdense object that forms from the collapse of an average-size star.

Mary A. Barnes and Kathleen Duey, *The Ultimate Asteroid Book: The Inside Story on the Threat from the Skies.* New York: Aladdin Paperbacks, 1998. An excellent introduction to asteroids and how they pose a potential threat to Earth.

Pam Beasant, *1000 Facts About Space.* New York: Kingfisher Books, 1992. An informative collection of basic facts about the stars, planets, asteroids, and other heavenly bodies.

Heather Couper and Nigel Henbest, *Black Holes.* London: Dorling Kindersley, 1996. A handsomely illustrated book that explains in easy terms for young people the basic concepts surrounding black holes and their deep gravity wells.

Robert Gardner, *Science Project Ideas About the Moon.* Berkeley Heights, NJ: Enslow, 1997. An excellent collection of ideas for student projects about the moon.

Nigel Henbest, *DK Space Encyclopedia.* London: Dorling Kindersley, 1999. This beautifully mounted and critically acclaimed book is the best general source available for grade-school readers about the wonders of space.

Maria B. Jacobs and Nancy Ellwood, *Why Do the Oceans Have Tides?* New York: Rosen Publishing

Group, 1999. Explains the workings of one of the major ways that gravity affects Earth.

Don Nardo, *The Solar System.* San Diego: KidHaven Press, 2002. This colorfully illustrated book describes the various members of the sun's family. The book ends by examining the probability that the solar system will eventually be absorbed by the giant black hole lurking in the center of our galaxy.

Steve Parker, *Isaac Newton and Gravity.* New York: Chelsea House, 1995. A clearly written, informative biography of Newton, including how he formulated his famous theory of gravity.

Gregory L. Vogt, *Asteroids, Comets, and Meteors.* Brookfield, CT: Millbrook Press, 1996. Tells the basic facts about these stony, metallic, and/or icy bodies orbiting the sun.

Index

About the Author

In addition to his acclaimed volumes on ancient civilizations, historian Don Nardo has published several studies of modern scientific discoveries and phenomena. Among these are *The Extinction of the Dinosaurs*; *Cloning*; *Atoms*; volumes about the asteroids, the moon, Neptune, and Pluto; and a biography of the noted scientist Charles Darwin. Mr. Nardo lives with his wife Christine in Massachusetts.